SWAP
How Trade Works

SWAP
How Trade Works

Philip I. Levy and Claude Barfield

AEI Press
Publisher for the American Enterprise Institute
Washington, D.C.

Distributed by arrangement with the National Book Network
15200 NBN Way, Blue Ridge Summit, PA 17214
To order call toll free 1-800-462-6420 or 1-717-794-3800.

For all other inquiries please contact AEI Press, 1150 17th Street,
N.W., Washington, D.C. 20036 or call 1-800-862-5801.

Levy, Philip I.
    Swap : how trade works / Philip I. Levy and Claude Barfield.
        p. cm.
    Includes bibliographical references.
    ISBN-13: 978-0-8447-7206-6 (pbk.)
    ISBN-10: 0-8447-7206-2 (pbk.)
    ISBN-13: 978-0-8447-7207-3 (ebook)
    ISBN-10: 0-8447-7207-0 (ebook)
    1. United States—Commerce. 2. International trade. I. Barfield,
    Claude E. II. Title.
    HF1455.L45 2011
    382.0973—dc23

CONTENTS

LIST OF ILLUSTRATIONS

ACKNOWLEDGMENTS

The authors would like to thank Dharana Rijal and Tobias Baude for excellent research support in the completion of this study.

1

SPECIALIZATION
AND TRADE

Few who read this book will go on to become subsistence farmers, grow their own food, sew their own clothes, and whittle branches for entertainment. Not that there's anything wrong with all that.

Instead, readers will likely specialize and trade. You may grow cash crops as farmers; produce machine tools in factories; or provide health care to your fellow citizens. We rarely think about how dependent each of these vocations is on trade. As valuable as machine tools may be, you cannot eat them, nor wear them, nor live in them. The only way a factory worker is able to meet her basic needs is to trade the machine tools she produces for other goods and services.

In a rudimentary economy, our worker would barter her tools directly for eggs or cloth. In a modern economy, she would receive money for her work, which is easier to store and significantly less fragile than eggs. But it is the same basic idea either way.

It is not hard to see the gains from specialization. If a child breaks his wrist in a fall, we would not be satisfied to have it treated by the class teacher, nor the school nurse, nor even a family doctor. We would want the child seen by an orthopedist, someone who specializes in understanding the intricacies of how bones function and mend. If there are to be such specialists, someone else will need to grow their food and build their houses. The idea that individuals will specialize and be more productive is central to how modern economies function and advance.

The economist Angus Maddison provides some striking numbers about just how far specialization and trade have brought us.[1] If we compare the United States in 1820 to the United States in 2001, early Americans were more self-sufficient, worked harder, and earned less. In 1820, they worked an average of 968 hours per person per year, versus 770 in 2001. But for each working hour, the early Americans produced $1.49 worth of goods and services in 1820, compared to $28.59 in 2001 (a comparison that accounts for inflation).

Of course, some of this growth came from great discoveries, such as how to harness electricity, how to use engines for locomotion, and how to produce disease-resistant and well-fertilized crops. Yet even such discoveries came from the specialization of scientists and inventors.

What, you may ask, does any of this have to do with international trade, with current account deficits, with trade agreements and commercial disputes? The principle is the same. Countries can specialize in producing those goods and services they can make at their lowest cost and trade with other countries for mutual gain.

Although the underlying principle of specialization and market exchange may be the same, there are some important differences when we trade across international borders rather than trading across towns.

Perhaps the foremost difference is that it is much easier to intervene internationally. Countries can apply taxes to goods when they cross their borders. Such import taxes, known as tariffs, were once quite common and quite high. The economic historian Doug Irwin writes of "The Great Tariff Debate of 1888" when tariff revenue amounted to more than 30 percent of the value of U.S. imports. This raised the price of goods produced abroad, and so Americans bought fewer of them.[2]

At the time, Democrats were eager to cut tariffs because the government had too much revenue (imagine!), while Republicans wanted to maintain them so as to protect domestic producers from import competition. For our purposes, it is the desire for protection, to shield businesses from foreign competitors, that is most interesting.

For anyone running a business, life is much easier without competition. There is less pressure to keep prices low or to innovate. When there is competition, there will be businesses that lose. Of course, consumers have the opposite interests. Domestically, consumer interests have often won out. New competition brings cheaper food, new products, and better services. We have antitrust laws to encourage competition, and the Constitution prohibits states from erecting barriers to commerce between them. Sometimes that has meant brutal and painful competition, as in the twentieth century when the textile industry of the northeastern United States was largely replaced by textile firms in the Southeast.

In international trade, there is nothing to match the constitutional prohibition on interstate trade barriers, and consumer interests are less politically potent. Over time, in the wake of damaging episodes of protectionism, countries have reached agreements to reduce and cap the sorts of barriers they erect against each other. Such agreements, like the global General Agreement on Tariffs and Trade (GATT) or the continental North American Free Trade Agreement (NAFTA), have been politically controversial and wield nothing like the force of the U.S. Constitution. Nor are they comprehensive in their support for free trade. Exceptions abound, and pressures to protect domestic producers increase in difficult economic times.

Thus, in comparing domestic and international competition, the same gains from specialization and competition apply, but it is both easier and more tempting for governments to intervene internationally. It is not impossible to block domestic commercial transactions, just harder. Because domestic and international competition share the same market principles, trade can serve as a prime battleground for debates about the merits of free markets and free enterprise.

The astute reader, at this point, may begin to wonder whether this depiction of trade—as international specialization and competition—has anything to do with the sort of trade depicted in the newspapers or on the web. There, the discussion concerns jobs lost, or unfair practices abroad, or soaring deficits, or decisions by heavily acronymed international organizations. A major purpose of this book will be to connect the abstract vision of trade with its portrayal in the daily media, thereby providing a guide to important policy debates.

The next chapter grapples with the question of who specializes in what. It will discuss the idea of comparative advantage, one of the more powerful and less intuitive ideas in economics. It will also ask why Europe ships cars to the United States and the United States ships other cars right back to Europe, which seems to fly in the face of arguments about specialization. It will also consider what it means when specialization is due to another government's policies, not just natural factors such as land and weather.

Chapter 3 asks whether and how trade helps Americans. It asks whether globalization, in the form of trade, inexorably drives down wages or destroys jobs. Although there are certainly losers from global competition, the chapter shows that trade is sometimes blamed when other forces—such as domestic competition or new technologies—are really at play. It recounts the remarkable record of growth and prosperity that have accompanied America's increasing openness to world trade.

Chapter 4 turns around the question of the preceding chapter and asks what trade does for trading partners, particularly in the developing world. Popular campaigns for "fair trade" often either imply or state outright that trade exploits the cheap labor of poorer countries. In contrast, trade's advocates argue that it is indispensable in fostering economic growth.

In these chapters' discussion of whether trade helps or hurts, the judgment is based on whether people enjoy better jobs or higher wages. That can be a difficult measure to observe. A poor but common proxy is to use trade deficits as a way to keep score—the gap between the value of goods a country ships abroad and those it imports. That is the subject of chapter 5. It draws a sharp distinction between trade imbalances with a single partner, such as China, and trade imbalances with the rest of the globe. In neither case does the trade deficit emerge as a very good measure of trade policy success or national well-being.

Chapter 6 considers some of the many ways that governments intervene in trade and their effects on ordinary people. For example, if one country slaps a tariff on another's exports, who ends up paying that tariff? And if tariffs serve to protect domestic producers and raise revenue, why, then, do we see a dizzying array of other types of trade barriers?

To this point, we have treated trade as a simple exchange of goods across borders. Modern trade is more complex, and that complexity is controversial. Countries trade not just goods but also services, such as engineering and banking. It is exceedingly common for trade to occur between two parts of the same multinational corporation, thus adding international investment into the mix. The ability to trade can be blocked not just by border barriers but also by carefully crafted domestic regulation. Chapter 7 looks at such trade issues inside the borders.

Chapter 8 deals with some of the institutions of international trade, especially the World Trade Organization (WTO) and its predecessor, the General Agreement on Tariffs and Trade. Such agreements have raised apprehensions about the loss of national sovereignty. Just how powerful are these bodies, and why have they been proliferating?

Chapter 9 focuses on two issues that have become increasingly prominent in public discussions of trade in the United States: labor and the environment. The extent to which these issues are relevant to trade and belong in trade agreements has been the main fissure splitting what was once a bipartisan coalition supporting trade liberalization.

The last chapter discusses the often challenging interaction between the economics and politics of trade. It will return to the theme of this one, that the basic argument for gains from trade is the argument for free and unfettered market exchange. It also addresses the policy challenges ahead for free trade.

2

**COMPARATIVE
ADVANTAGE**

Imagine you have a room full of people, and you want to quickly separate the trade economists from the normal folk. Just climb up on a soapbox and declare: "I'm worried about our country's declining competitiveness. At the rate we're going, soon nothing will be made here, and everything will be made abroad. Who's with me?" Trade economists will scoff and shake their heads. Pretty much everyone else will likely join you.

To trade economists, you will just have abandoned one of the central precepts of their art, the principle of comparative advantage. As legend has it, the great economist Paul Samuelson was once asked for an idea in economics that was both universally true and not obvious. His reply: comparative advantage.

Perhaps the biggest obstacle to grasping comparative advantage in the real world lies with trade deficits and trade surpluses. For that reason, let us set them aside right now and come back to them in chapter 5. For the moment, we will require that our trading countries always have balanced trade.

For the moment, let us think of two countries and call them Ruritania and Industria. To make the discussion simple, we will say that each country produces only two products: wool and looms. Being advanced folk, we will put ourselves in the position of Industria before it ever starts to trade and explore trade possibilities.

The first question we want to ask is: How much do wool and looms cost? Presumably, if they cost less abroad, we may have a reason to trade. Here we come to the crux of how trade economists are different. A normal person is tempted to answer: "Looms cost $96," or "Wool runs $8 per unit." A trade economist will say that money is a distraction here. We are talking about a world that has only two goods. The only way you can persuade someone to give you wool is to give them a loom in exchange (or vice versa).

So a meaningful answer might be: down at the Industria central market, it takes 12 units of wool to get 1 loom. Thus, a loom *costs* 12 units of wool. This is known as a relative price. We can calculate them even if we start from dollar prices:

$$\frac{\textbf{\$96 PER LOOM}}{\textbf{\$8 PER WOOL UNIT}} = \textbf{12 WOOL PER LOOM}$$

Word then comes in from abroad that in Ruritania, a loom costs 20 units of wool. It might be that in Ruritania, a loom costs $600 and wool costs $30; it is the relative price that matters. If we put everything in terms of wool cost, looms are relatively cheap in Industria and relatively expensive in Ruritania.

If the two countries started to trade with each other, Ruritanians looking to buy looms would prefer to buy them in Industria. They would offer their wool in exchange. They would meet a willing counterpart in the Industrial wool shoppers; for them, instead of getting only 12 units of wool per loom, they might get up to 20.

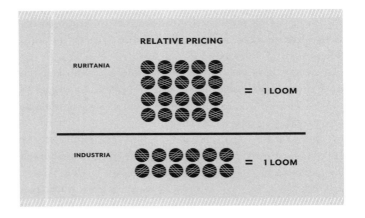

In Industria, the supply of wool would increase, as would the demand for looms. This would bid up the relative price of looms. Back in Ruritania, the demand for wool would increase, as would the supply of looms. This would push down the relative price of looms.

This incentive to trade would continue until the relative price was the same in both countries, perhaps at 16 units of wool per loom. Thus, we have an example of trade: Industria has a *comparative advantage* in looms (a low relative price) and sends them to Ruritania in exchange for wool, in which Ruritania has a comparative advantage.

The dollar prices in this example were meaningless. There is no reason to think that the two countries would use the same currency. Suppose, instead, that the dollar figures above represent the number of worker hours it took to produce wool or looms. This is in line with the reasoning of David Ricardo, who came up with this idea back in the early 1800s.[3]

In this case, we can imagine someone standing on a Ruritanian soapbox and warning about the dangers of trade with Industria. "Look," they might say, "Industria can produce a unit of wool in 8 hours, rather than our 30. It can produce a loom in 96 hours, rather than our 600. How can we possibly compete? They will undersell us on everything!"

In the vernacular, the Ruritanian rabble-rouser just made an argument based on *absolute advantage*. In terms of labor costs, Industria has an absolute advantage in both wool and looms. But it has a *comparative advantage* only in looms.

Both approaches sound plausible. Which is right?

Imagine the scene when a Ruritanian believer in absolute advantage shows up at the Industria central market. "Everything is so cheap here! Give me a dozen units of wool and a loom, please."

To which the Industrial merchant replies, "OK. And how will you be paying for that?"

Now our Ruritanian has a problem. There are only two goods, so he has to offer either wool or a loom, and those goods would have to be made back in Ruritania. The fundamental problem with the idea that one country will undersell the other in every good is that the undersold country would have no way to pay. Comparative advantage relies on the idea of exchange, and therefore payment is not a problem.

All we needed for comparative advantage to work was that the countries had different relative prices before they started to trade (the time before trade is known as *autarky*). We have not said much yet about where those different relative prices might come from. We gave just one example, in which it took different lengths of time to produce the goods in the different countries. That would be classified as a *technology* argument for why countries trade. Ruritanian technology determined how many hours it took for a worker to produce a loom or wool.

That's not the only reason two countries might trade. Ruritania and Industria might have exactly the same technologies, but different *endowments*. Ruritania might have vast expanses of good grazing land, but relatively few people. Industria might have a large population and large deposits of iron ore. Even if they had access to the same blueprints for looms, the resources could mean that Ruritania found it relatively cheap to produce sheep.

Alternatively, the two countries could be identical in their technologies and their endowments, but have different *tastes*. The Ruritanians might just have an inordinate passion for looms that would drive up their relative price.

Much of trade thinking delves into these different possibilities for the root cause of trade. Which scenario applies can make a big difference if we want to think about such questions as technology transfer policy or what trade will do to worker wages and land rents. But as a basic explanation for why and what countries trade, comparative advantage will usually suffice. Countries export goods they produce relatively cheaply and import goods that are relatively expensive. The word "relatively" is the key to that conclusion and to understanding comparative advantage.

Although this conception of trade is very abstract—two countries, two goods, no money, balanced trade—it provides some exceedingly useful insights that carry through. We can take one step in the direction of realism if we introduce a twist on our story. Suppose that the Ruritanian Governing Central Policy Committee, for ideological reasons, issues an inviolable decree: all Ruritanian enterprises must henceforth sell or buy looms at a price of 16 units of wool.

Ruritanian trade is no longer the exclusive outcome of "natural" causes, such as technology, endowments, or tastes. It is shaped by government intervention. So what does this mean for the freedom-loving folk in Industria? Remarkably little. As far as the Industrials are concerned, trade is a different and more efficient way of transforming looms into wool. They send off looms to Ruritania and instead of getting back 12 units of wool per loom (the autarky price), they get back 16 units (in our assumed free-trade price). That's the best way available to turn looms into wool. From a simple economic standpoint, it makes no difference whether the transformation at the other end of the trade is natural or unnatural. All that mattered was the relative price. The new opportunity offered by trade left the people of Industria better off—more warmly dressed—than they would have been in isolation.

Whatever the motivation for trade, the next chapter asks whether in practice it has made the people of the United States better off.

3

THE IMPACT ON AMERICAN WORKERS AND THE ECONOMY

These days, trade concerns are usually raised amid broader discussions of globalization. Although the meaning of that term is malleable, globalization usually describes the process by which advances in technology, transportation, and communications are producing ever tighter integration of national economies and cultures. Trade is at the center of this process, but it is accompanied by the spread of technology, foreign investment, capital flows, and migration. On all these fronts, globalization has accelerated in recent decades.

We see the results all around us: in lamb from New Zealand and Australia competing with lamb from California and Texas for space on American restaurant menus; in construction machinery from Caterpillar and General Electric utilized to build huge dams in China; and in General Motors and Ford auto plants in Europe, while BMW, Toyota, Honda, and Hyundai factories and assembly lines dot the U.S. landscape. Meanwhile, news, gossip, and culture race around the world via Twitter and Facebook.

Such rapid change can be unsettling and disruptive, both for individuals and for societies. This chapter and the next tally up some of the benefits and the costs.

The United States holds a unique position in the global economy: it is both the world's largest national economy and the largest trading nation, with a gross domestic product (GDP) of just over $14 trillion and exports and imports together amounting to about $2.4 trillion in 2009.[4] With the United States being geographically large and blessed with substantial natural and agricultural resources and highly diversified regions, its economy is more self-contained than other major trading nations in Europe and Asia. For instance, as recently as 1970, total U.S. trade, both exports and imports of goods and services, amounted to only about 10 percent of U.S. output (figure 3-1). By 2007, this total had almost tripled to 30 percent of total U.S. output of

FIGURE 3-1. U.S. TRADE IN GOODS AND SERVICES AS A PERCENTAGE OF GDP

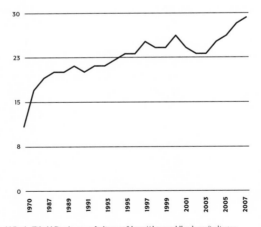

Source: World Bank, "World Development Indicators," http://data.worldbank.org/indicator.

goods and services. Still, even today about 85 percent of the goods and services consumed by American businesses and individuals are generated right here at home.

Though its economy is more self-contained than many others' national economies, the United States has not escaped a vigorous debate over the impact of international trade and investment on U.S. workers and businesses—particularly the effects on jobs and income.

"THE GIANT SUCKING SOUND": U.S. WORKERS AND TRADE WITH DEVELOPING COUNTRIES

The perils of trade, in the eyes of many skeptics, lie in exchanges with less developed economies that have lower wages than the United States, In fact, U.S. trade is still predominantly with advanced, high-income economies,

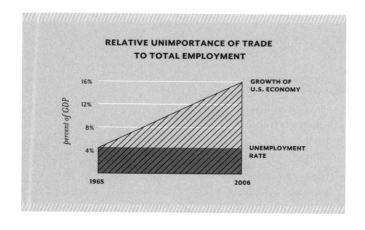

RELATIVE UNIMPORTANCE OF TRADE
TO TOTAL EMPLOYMENT

but trade with lower-income developing countries is increasing rapidly. For instance, Mexico, whose per capita income is just over $13,000 (compared to $46,000 for the United States) is the United States' third-largest trading partner.[5] Thus, as far back as the North American Free Trade Agreement in 1994, critics of U.S. free-trade policies and of globalization warned of a "giant sucking sound" of U.S. jobs being lost to Mexico and other low-income countries.

In fact, trade has little impact on *total* employment in the United States. The most important factors determining job creation are population growth, the percentage of Americans in the workforce, and domestic economic policies that affect the business cycle and the functioning of labor markets (figure 3-2). Demonstrating the relative unimportance of trade to total employment, from 1965 to 2006, the share of imports in the U.S. economy rose from 4.4 to 16.0 percent of GDP; yet during that same time period, employment almost doubled, and the average unemployment rate was about 4.5 percent at both the beginning and the end of that period. [6]

The best way to understand the process of job gains and losses is to think of the U.S. economy as a giant churn. At home, new technologies emerge, and consumer tastes and fashions come and go. These dynamics combine with competition from abroad to produce job shifts among specific sectors. Jobs are continuously created and destroyed. As an example, in the decade 1996–2006,

FIGURE 3-2. LABOR FORCE AND EMPLOYMENT, 1947–2007

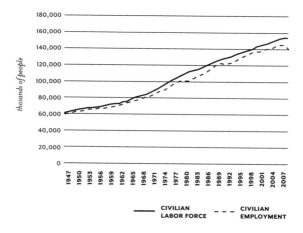

Source: Bureau of Labor Statistics, U.S. Department of Labor, http://www.bls.gov/

sixteen million private-sectors jobs were lost each year; however, during that same period, seventeen million new jobs were created annually, resulting in a net gain of about one million jobs per year. As Federal Reserve chairman Benjamin Bernanke has asserted: "The U.S. labor market exhibits a phenomenal capacity for creative destruction."[7]

WAGES AND INCOME INEQUALITY

What of the specter of a "race to the bottom" as we try to compete with nations such as China with average wages only a tenth of U.S. wages? China (per capita income, $6600) now supplies almost 20 percent of total U.S. imports.[8] Such a descent might occur if the United States and China (and other low-income countries) competed for only one product or sector. But the United States and other countries compete across numerous industries and occupations; and through the specialization described in the previous chapter, in sectors where the United States has a comparative advantage, the wages of its workers can and do remain far above those of Chinese workers. The key here is the productive capacity of U.S. workers versus the workers of other nations. Competitors from abroad must contend with the higher education and greater technical skills of U.S. workers, as well as their access to superior technology and efficiently functioning capital, labor, and investment markets. Furthermore, historically the growth of a nation's average wages is determined by productivity growth. As the accompanying figure (figure 3-3) illustrates, increases in worker compensation over time almost perfectly match productivity growth.

This is also true, of course, with developing countries, as China's recent wage and productivity history clearly demonstrates—from 1997 to 2007, average real wages tripled, according to government data, reflecting a concomitant rise in the skills and productivity of Chinese workers.[9] Still, the average worker in a Chinese factory is not designing new telecommunications equipment or working in a biotech lab. Often only several years off a farm, where they attained only a primary school

FIGURE 3-3. LABOR PRODUCTIVITY AND REAL COMPENSATION PER HOUR (NONFARM BUSINESS SECTOR)

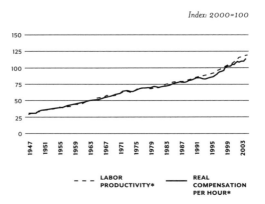

Index: 2000=100

LABOR PRODUCTIVITY*   REAL COMPENSATION PER HOUR*

*Output per hour of all persons. **Compensation per hour divided by the implicit price deflator for nonfarm business output.
Source: Bureau of Labor Statistics, U.S. Department of Labor, http://www.bls.gov/

education, most Chinese workers are still engaged in turning out apparel, shoes, and toys, along with low-end manufactured goods, such as radios, television sets, and DVDs.

Though trade does not explain total job growth in the United States (or other countries), it does have an impact on employment in particular sectors. U.S. comparative advantage tends to lead to exports of more skill-intensive products, such as aircraft, construction machinery, chemicals, pharmaceuticals, and medical devices. Conversely, trade can reduce jobs in low-wage, low-skilled sectors, such as textiles and shoes. But the real story here, in light of the political controversies, is not that trade destroys high-wage jobs in manufacturing. More accurately, trade has decreased low-wage, so-called bad jobs in manufacturing because, in general, import-competing sectors pay well below U.S. average wages, while our chief manufacturing export industries pay wages that are far above average. In 1999, the average hourly wage in the apparel industry was 36 percent below average manufacturing wages.[10]

Of even greater significance, domestic and international competition, along with technological change, have increased demand for more highly educated, skilled workers, resulting in an increasing wage premium for such employees. In the United States, one study concluded that between 1980 and 2005, wages of college graduates rose 22 percent relative to high school graduates, this despite a large increase in the number of college graduates in the workforce.[11] In sum, a substantial amount of research suggests that trade plays only a small role in rising income inequality compared to the major impact of new technologies that create much greater demand for ever higher worker skill levels.

TRADE AND SOCIETAL RESPONSIBILITY

For the laid-off worker, it does not matter much whether he lost his job because of low-wage competition from abroad, because of a new competitor in a neighboring state, or because a computer-guided machine tool can now perform his old task more cheaply. Whatever the ultimate causes, what can be done to counter the social disruption for U.S. workers and their families? Attempts to restrict trade through tariffs or quotas, though often politically popular, offer little help. Though trade protection may temporarily stem job losses in a particular sector, it also imposes higher costs on the wider economy, through higher costs to consumers (who are also workers) and to U.S. firms that must pay inflated prices for parts and components affected by tariffs or quotas. The costs of protection almost invariably outweigh the benefits. In a study of twenty-one sectors, analysts found that, on average, high tariffs, quotas, and other restrictive measures cost the U.S. public $170,000 for each job "saved."[12]

Furthermore, given the structure of U.S. tariffs, the result is most damaging to low-income workers, who spend a large proportion of their wages on basics. Staple consumer products, such as apparel and shoes, face import taxes over 30 percent, thus taking a large bite out of low-income household expenditures.

A more effective set of alternatives would key on retraining and educating displaced workers, as well as shoring up the national social safety net. In early 2009, the U.S. Congress passed the largest trade adjustment assistance program in the nation's history, including extended benefits for employees displaced by trade and job retraining programs. In addition, in the future, economywide proposals aimed at all displaced workers—not just those who have lost their jobs allegedly by import competition—should be explored. One proposal would be to provide time-limited wage insurance whereby workers would receive partial compensation when they were reemployed at a job paying less than the previous wage. Because the compensation would come only on reemployment, this would preserve the incentive to reenter the workforce. Other proposals along this line—cushioning the social costs of job loss while preserving employment incentives—include legislation to increase the portability of health and pension benefits, allowing these forms of compensation to move with the worker and thus reducing the worries associated with the "churn" of job loss and creation.

There is no question that trade liberalization and globalization create both winners and losers. But on balance, the positive results for Americans far outweigh the costs. Economists at the nonpartisan Peterson Institute for International Economics in Washington, D.C., recently found that a half century of steady trade and investment liberalization has generated an increase of U.S. income of roughly $1 trillion per year, which translates into about $10,000 for the typical American family.[13]

4

**DOES TRADE
HELP OUR TRADING
PARTNERS?**

We have explored the benefits of international trade and investment for the United States, but what about our trading partners, particularly lower-income developing countries? Are U.S. gains coming through the exploitation of downtrodden workers abroad?

Some historical context will help. In 1945, much of the developed world—Europe and Japan—lay in ruins, with economies that had been physically devastated by the war. The even larger developing world (excluding the Soviet bloc and China, which for forty years would remain isolated from international trade and investment) was just emerging from a colonial past (Africa, Asia, and the Middle East) or starting from a per capita base (Latin America).

U.S. TRADE WITH THE DEVELOPED WORLD

In the first postwar decade, partly in response to the onset of the Cold War and partly in response to the firm belief that more open markets and deeper trade relations would foster democratic values and, ultimately, more peaceful relations among nations, the United States embarked on a twofold international economic policy. First, through the Marshall Plan and other programs, it provided major support for rebuilding the economies of Europe, and of Germany and Japan, its former enemies. Second, it took the lead, through both unilateral measures and international agreements, in constructing a new, rules-based international trading system, overseen by the General Agreement on Tariffs and Trade.

This system, though not perfect, did provide a secure framework for both developed and later developing nations to let trade and specialization begin to work their magic in inducing greater economic growth. For instance, U.S. border tariffs (i.e., taxes on imports) were systematically and quickly lowered from an average of more than 40 percent in the postwar period down to less than 10 percent by the end of the 1950s, providing global opportunities at a crucial early juncture for access to the

FIGURE 4-1. CHANGES IN TARIFF RATES SINCE THE LATE 1980S

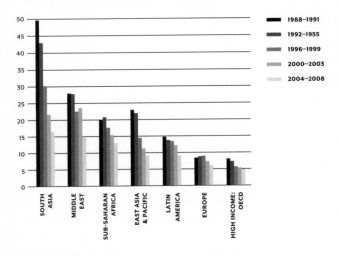

Source: World Bank, "World Development Indicators" and "Global Development Finance," http://data. worldbank.org/.

huge U.S. market. Subsequently, through numerous rounds of negotiations, worldwide tariff rates steeply declined (figure 4-1). Today, U.S. average tariff rates are 3 percent, while those of Europe and Japan are 1.5 and 2.3 percent, respectively.[14]

U.S. TRADE WITH DEVELOPING COUNTRIES

In addition, during the early postwar decades, the U.S. economy constituted more than half of world output, and U.S. consumers (through imports) soaked up much of the output of foreign economies. Thus, particularly for developing countries as they entered world trade and markets, the U.S. economy provided a strong boost for growth. The U.S. economy remains a major market for foreign products, with imports totaling $1.4 trillion in 2009.

Trade liberalization in developing countries was slower to emerge, as many of these countries were long attracted to Marxist state-controlled economic organization, in particular so-called dependency theory. This theory was based on the highly influential work of Raul Prebisch, an Argentinian economist whose ideas dominated development policy at the United Nations for several decades.[15] Prebisch argued that, contrary to theories of Adam Smith and David Ricardo, open trade policies would not lead to specialization and higher growth. Instead, Ruritania (developing countries) would be doomed to perpetual dependency on developed countries because prices for the raw materials (agricultural goods and minerals) they produced would continue to be driven down through competition, while the price of manufacturing goods from developed countries would increase, not least because of industrial monopolies. For Prebisch and a number of national leaders from the developing world, the only way out of this alleged trap was an "import substitution" policy, or rapid, forced industrialization through a mix of trade protection and subsidies to foster "infant industries."

Unfortunately, in practice the implementation of such policies almost always produced a wasteful competition for government handouts, combined with increased corruption and collusion between government officials and local private business interests. Protection sealed off many developing economies from foreign technology, investment, and managerial know-how.

Brazil provides a graphic example of the negative effects of an import substitution policy. From the late 1970s through most of the 1980s, Brazil adopted an "informatics policy" that closed its markets to foreign computer and software manufacturers with the aim of creating national information industries. Coming just as personal computers and software design were taking off around the world, the results were disastrous for Brazil's competitiveness. It effectively cut off the nation from the latest technology and set back for almost a decade the modernization through computerization of Brazil's manufacturing and services companies. In 1990, when Brazil scrapped the whole system, its minister of economy ruefully admitted: "We are effectively very backward because of this stupid nationalism."[16]

Meanwhile, beginning in the late 1960s, a new paradigm for development emerged, led by a small group of developing economies in East Asia: Hong Kong, South Korea, Taiwan, and, later, Thailand, Malaysia, and Indonesia. Rather than joining the herd pursuing the import substitution model, these countries adopted export promotion policies and a gradual opening of their economies to import competition and foreign investment. Domestically, these countries also utilized the profits from trade to invest heavily in human and physical capital—that is, schools and roads.

For individual national economies, the results were dramatic. Between 1960 and 2000, Taiwan, South Korea, Singapore, and Hong Kong had GDP per capita growth rates of 5 to 6 percent, while the relatively closed trade and investment markets of Bolivia, Ghana, and Venezuela had *no* per capita income growth over the same period.[17]

The Asian success story had ripple effects. By the late 1980s a number of developing countries were moving toward more open trade and investment regimes. Indeed, during the 1980s and 1990s, there was a wave of unilateral trade reforms, with the result that average tariff rates for developing countries dropped by half: from 30 percent in the early 1980s to 15 percent by the year 2000 (in 2009, this average had dropped further to 12.3 percent).[18] Concomitantly, political leaders from the developing world, who had long been deeply suspicious of multinational corporations and foreign direct investment, now saw foreign direct investment (FDI) as one key to higher economic growth and technological advance.

Recent research by two World Bank economists, David Dollar and Aart Kraay, has provided a direct comparison of the economic growth and per capita income record of those developing countries that both undertook the greatest tariff reduction policies since 1980 and had great increase in trade volume in relation to GDP (the "globalizers," as the author label them) with other developing countries ("non-globalizers") and with rich developed countries. Their results are striking: rich-country growth rates have slowed down over the past decade, after increasing during the 1970s and 1980s. This is also the pattern followed by non-globalizing developing countries. On the other hand, the globalizers have followed a very different pattern by accelerating growth during the entire period of the 1970s, the 1980s, and the 1990s. The economists conclude: "In the 1990s, the globalizing developing countries grew at 5.0% *per capita*, rich countries at 2.2%, and non-globalizing developing countries at only 1.4%. Thus, the globalizers are catching up with rich countries while the non-globalizers fall further and further behind."[19]

Contrary to dependency theory, trade liberalization did not condemn developing countries to low-value commodities and raw materials; rather, it produced a major transformation in the specialization of developing countries. In 1950, agricultural commodities and minerals constituted more than 80 percent of developing country trade, with manufacturing making up only 15 percent. By 2001, manufacturing products made up more than 80 percent of developing country exports, with agricultural exports and minerals dropping to about 10 percent each (figure 4-2).

FIGURE 4-2. SHARES IN MERCHANDISE EXPORTS OF DEVELOPING COUNTRIES

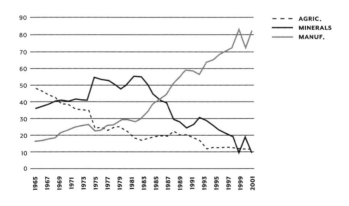

Source: World Bank, "World Development Indicators," GTAP Version 5 Database, http://data.worldbank.org/.

FIGURE 4-3. GROWTH IN THE VOLUME OF WORLD MERCHANDISE TRADE AND GDP

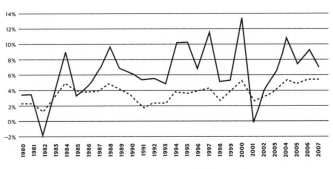

– – – **GROSS DOMESTIC PRODUCT, CONSTANT PRICES**
——— **EXPORT VOLUME OF GOODS**

Source: International Monetary Fund, "IMF World Economic Outlook Database, April 2010," available at
http://www.imf.org/external/pubs/ft/weo/2010/01/weodata/index.aspx.

One important result of this liberalization was that trade became a key factor in overall economic growth for many nations. From the mid-1960s to the present time, trade volumes far outpaced world production almost every year: between 1945 and 2000, world GDP grew sixfold while trade expanded sixteenfold.[20] Thus trade provided a powerful boost to national GDP and per capita income growth for those nations that entered world markets (figure 4-3).

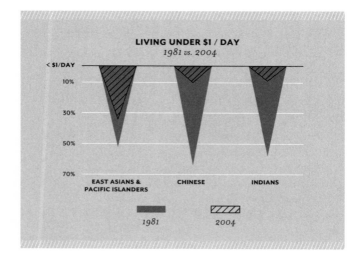

The spread of trade and investment liberalization throughout much of the developing world also was a key factor in a dramatic reduction in poverty rates. Between 1981 and 2004, the percentage of developing country populations living on $1 per day (a standard measure of poverty) decreased from 40 percent to 18 percent (and those living on $2 per day, from 67 percent to 48percent). To fully comprehend what was going on, one must go behind these overall numbers. For instance, given the range of policies described above, it is no surprise that there were regional differences: East Asian and the Pacific nations witnessed the greatest declines in poverty: from 58 percent below $1 per day in 1981, down to 9 percent in 2004. Within Asia, the huge populations of China and India dominate the shift: China, 64 percent down to 10 percent, and India, 52 percent down to 34 percent.[21]

Sadly, sub-Saharan Africa—wracked by civil wars, lawlessness, corruption, and misguided policies—saw virtually no decrease in $1 per day poverty: 42 percent to 41 percent between 1981 and 2004. Furthermore, given population growth, over this period there was an absolute increase in the number of sub-Saharan Africans living below the poverty line: from 167 million to 298 million. Though there are a number of reasons for Africa's poor record over the past five decades, much of the blame lies in development strategies that combined excessive dependence on foreign aid with closed economies and infant industry dreams. Foreign aid can reinforce sound policies, but when combined with high barriers that shut out foreign competition and technology, it can deter needed reforms, as well as foster bloated public bureaucracies, corruption, and perverse fiscal and currency policies. Signs of hope have appeared recently. Countries such as Botswana, Mozambique, and Uganda have achieved high growth rates (above 5 percent) since the late 1990s, through a mix of internal reforms, physical infrastructure development, sound fiscal policies, and more open trade and investment regimes.[22]

THE ISSUE OF "SWEATSHOPS"

Earnest, high-minded reformers and nongovernment organizations (NGOs) (often in alliance with college and university student groups) in the developed world have mounted numerous campaigns against "sweatshops," or plants that allegedly pay subsistence wages and force workers to toil for long hours, often dawn to dusk. They have also decried the destruction of rural, agricultural communities, lamenting that workers in Mexico or Vietnam have been shoved into dehumanizing urban environments.

Several years ago, Paul Krugman, winner of the Nobel Prize for economics, penned a sobering but honest rejoinder to the "moral outrage" voiced by opponents of globalization. It was titled "In Praise of Cheap Labor: Bad Jobs at Bad Wages Are Better Than No Jobs at All."[23]

Krugman took aim at social activists' highly romanticized view of life in agrarian communities. He pointed out that rather than basking in a latter-day Garden of Eden, the typical agrarian peasant in Mexico or Vietnam toiled from before dawn until long after dusk, reaped virtually no profit from his small plot of land, and endured in a world without safe water, indoor toilet facilities, or minimal medical aid for his children. For all its downsides, the movement into industrial and commercial jobs was not a step backward but rather a first step toward greater prosperity. For the workers this was a rational decision.

Krugman candidly admitted that this was not a pretty

process. But he argued that improvements in living standards had not come mainly from foreign aid or the benign social policies of governments in developing countries. No, these changes were the "indirect and unintended result of the actions of soulless multinationals and rapacious local entrepreneurs, whose only concern was to take advantage of the profit opportunities offered by cheap labor. . . . But no matter how base the motives, the result has been to move hundreds of millions of people from abject poverty to something still awful but nonetheless significantly better." He concluded that the moral argument against globalization failed and was sustained only because opponents have "chosen not to think their position through."[24] Krugman's arguments have been strongly supported by Jeffrey Sachs, another distinguished economist who has long championed efforts to raise living standards in the developing world. At a joint appearance with Krugman at Harvard University he said, "My concern is not that there are too many sweatshops, but that there are too few."[25]

The track record of foreign aid in alleviating poverty is a very weak one. The track record of international trade in spurring growth and lifting people out of deprivation is quite strong. However, the first steps on that path to growth have often raised doubts among well-intentioned people in the developed world.

On the one hand, it can feel wrong for someone living in comfort to pay just a pittance to someone who sews clothes or harvests coffee beans. The commercial connection often creates a sense of responsibility in the affluent buyer—"Now that I'm dealing with this person, am I not obliged to see that she receives a higher wage?" The real question is whether that moral obligation exists only when there is a commercial transaction. If I stop paying a pittance to a worker in Vietnam and pay a higher wage to a more productive worker in Italy, is this a morally superior act? It does nothing to help the Vietnamese worker, who is still impoverished but now has fewer opportunities. It may help the Italian worker, but that worker was less needful to begin with.

So long as workers in developing countries are free to choose whether to accept a job offer with a multinational corporation, we know the additional opportunity can make them better off. *New York Times* columnist Nicholas Kristof, who has written extensively about working conditions in developing countries, reports that workers in developing countries consider employment in sweatshops as a dream job, compared to other employment opportunities. They consider it an "escalator" out of poverty.[26]

It is a matter of conscience for the well-off consumer whether they feel better offering such opportunities or taking their business to people who are less impoverished.

5

TRADE DEFICITS

The last two chapters asked whether trade is a boon or a bane for citizens in the United States and abroad. As we saw, there is no single indicator to track in the business pages to see whether we are winning or losing from trade. In fact, one of the great lessons of trade is that both sides to a trade can win; gains need not come at a partner's expense.

This insight can be elusive, however, and there is a very common tendency to reach for a more accessible substitute measure of trade success. The most common candidate as a measure is a country's trade balance. The persistent U.S. trade deficit is often held up as an indicator of national failing, while China's large trade surplus is taken as a measure of its economic achievement.

THE PREFERENCE FOR TRADE SURPLUSES

This preference for trade surpluses was at the heart of mercantilism, a school of thought that equated national power with a hoard of gold (or similar wealth). The pile of lucre, or so the thinking went, allowed the possessor to hire and equip armies, thereby translating fairly directly into national might.[27] British devotion to mercantilism in the late eighteenth century led to trade frictions with the American colonies that helped spark the American Revolution.[28]

How do we reconcile this line of thinking with our simple model of comparative advantage from chapter 2? In that chapter, our Ruritanians and our Industrials cared only about wool and looms. At the time, we did not even envision them having any money at all. We can remedy that now. Let us suppose that traders in either country can issue little green slips of paper called IOUs. We can go back to the scene in which a Ruritanian wished to purchase both wool and a loom from an Industrial. When the Industrial asks how the Ruritanian wishes to pay for all that, the Ruritanian can wave a fistful of IOUs at him.

What are the IOUs good for? They are good for wool or looms at some future date. Of course, back in the real world, the only reason anyone accepts U.S. dollars is that they can be exchanged for goods or services sometime in the future. If you sell someone a bicycle or a TV set in exchange for dollars, you give up something valuable on the understanding that you will be able to buy something else valuable later on.

Let's stick with our imaginary transaction for just a moment more. If Industria sells Ruritania some wool and a loom in exchange for IOUs, then Industria runs a trade surplus (the value of its exports exceeds the value of its nonexistent imports), and Ruritania runs a matching trade deficit. Essentially, Ruritania has borrowed the goods from Industria; the IOUs constitute a promise to pay them back later.

So who got the better of this deal? That's the same question as whether it is better to be a borrower or a lender, and there is no universal answer. When a student borrows to invest in her education, when a young couple takes out a mortgage to buy a home, or when an entrepreneur takes out a loan to start a business, these may be sound decisions that lead to prosperity. On the other hand, running up a credit card tab to finance a wild party or an exorbitant vacation is usually ill-advised.

THE CURRENT ACCOUNT

The analogy to how countries engage in international trade and finance is very close. The fullest measure of international transactions, the *current account*, encompasses trade in goods and services, as well as income from investments abroad and transfer payments. Table 5-1 gives a breakdown of the current account in 2009 for both the United States and China.[29]

TABLE 5-1. CURRENT ACCOUNT BALANCES IN 2009, UNITED STATES AND CHINA (BILLIONS OF U.S. DOLLARS)

| | TRADE BALANCE | | | EXTRAS | | CURRENT ACCOUNT BALANCE |
	Goods	*Services*	*Total Trade Balance*	*Income*	*Transfers*	
United States	-517.0	138.4	-378.6	89.0	-130.2	-419.8
China	249.3	-28.7	220.6	28.7	34.8	284.1

Source: International Monetary Fund, "IMF World Economic Outlook Database, April 2010," available at http://www.imf.org/external/pubs/ft/weo/2010/01/weodata/index.aspx.

For a country such as the United States, with a market-determined exchange rate, the *current account* mirrors the *capital account*.[30] The current account captures trade in goods and services, plus income from international investments and transfer payments sent to and from the country (e.g., from immigrants to family back in the home country). The capital account captures the sale of IOUs, though they are more formally known as "financial instruments." These consist of U.S. government debt (Treasury bonds and notes), corporate bonds, stocks, and exotic fare such as collateralized debt obligations.[31]

Thus, one can look at Table 5-1 and say that the United States is a net borrower and China is a net lender. But why? At the heart of public controversy over the trade deficit is a chicken-and-egg question: which came first? Did the United States set out to borrow from the world, inevitably resulting in a trade deficit? Or did trade policies dictate a U.S. deficit and in turn require borrowing to finance it? Knowing that the current account and the capital account must mirror each other does nothing to resolve this question of causality.

We can label the first story, in which borrowing comes first, as a macroeconomic story. It argues that a country's imports are largely determined by broad economic factors, such as national savings and the rate at which the country is growing. Its exports are set by the same factors at play in its trading-partner countries. Our second story would be a trade policy story in which government regulation of trade drives importing and exporting decisions, and global borrowing and lending just shift to accommodate. How could we determine whether macroeconomic factors or trade policies are really driving the deficit?

Ideally, we would set up an experiment in which macroeconomic conditions changed sharply while trade policies changed very little. If trade policies are the root determinant of trade deficits, then we should not see much change in the current account. If macroeconomic conditions are the driver, we could see some big swings.

We just lived through a painful experiment of this sort. In the global financial crisis that erupted in late 2008, economies slowed dramatically and savings increased, while trade policies remained largely fixed. The results strongly support the macroeconomic story. In a time of stable trade policies, the 2009 current account deficit of $420 billion marked a drop of more than 40 percent from the $706.1 billion deficit in 2008.[32]

This experience shows why trade deficits are a poor measure of whether the United States "wins" from free trade. The U.S. current account deficit was dramatically smaller in 2009 than 2008, but unemployment was substantially higher, and the nation felt distinctly less prosperous.

In this case, a shrinking trade deficit correlated with fewer jobs. That belies a disturbingly common argument in trade debates—that exports bring jobs and imports bring unemployment.[33] The argument is based on the idea that any goods not imported would be produced at home. But the United States enjoyed long stretches of "full employment" that coincided with current account deficits. Any new jobs would have been counteracted by policymakers wary of an overheated economy and inflation. Trade can do a great deal to determine the types of jobs in an economy, but it does little to set the overall level of employment. We return to this issue in chapter 9.

The astute reader who gazes long enough at Table 5-1 will glean another important fact: in 2009, the United States trade deficit was substantially larger than China's trade surplus. That is because we are comparing the two countries' trade balances against the entire world. That world contains plenty of other countries, so no two countries' balances need add up.

From an economic standpoint, it is the overall current account balance that is significant. From a political standpoint, there is an unhealthy and misguided fixation on bilateral trade deficits, in particular the one between the United States and China.

Whereas a global current account balance might indicate unwise national borrowing, there is no useful economic information in a bilateral deficit. To see this, imagine that the United States and China were both in overall balance (zero current accounts). But suppose China imported oil from the Middle East; the United States imported toys from China; and the Middle Eastern countries imported drilling equipment from the United States. Each region could be in overall balance, but each would run a bilateral trade deficit with one partner and a surplus with the other.

This is not just a hypothetical possibility; the interplay

between U.S. trading partners is important empirically. From 1996 to 2009, China's share of U.S. imports almost tripled, from 6.5 percent to 19 percent. Yet the share of U.S. imports from Asia (including China) has held roughly constant, actually falling from 38.8 percent to 37.6 percent over the same time period.[34]

An important part of China's successful integration into the world economy has been its ability to take over limited parts of the global production chain from its Asian neighbors. Thus, a good that used to be finished in Malaysia might now be partially completed there with the final 10 percent of value added in China. For bilateral U.S. trade statistics, that good would now be counted as a Chinese import rather than a Malaysian one. This can make bilateral statistics deeply misleading.

In contrast, overall trade or current account balances

can be a useful measure of economic activity, but they are a poor proxy for national well-being or the costs and benefits of trade.

6

TRADE POLICIES

What can a government do about trade? All kinds of things, as it turns out. In this chapter, we will focus on the best-known trade interventions, in which a government uses its control of the borders to affect trade flows. In the next chapter, we will take up policies that work behind the border.[35]

When a foreign exporter loads a product onto a ship and it sails into another country's port, it must pass through customs before it legally enters the country. An enlightened country might well choose to let the goods pass on through. Historically, though, countries have taken this opportunity to apply a tax. Taxes on imports are known as tariffs.

TARIFFS

The tariff inserts itself as a gap between what global merchants receive and what domestic consumers pay. Economists like to think about tariffs as a wedge between domestic and global prices because it sidesteps the tricky question of who pays the tariff. We won't shy from the challenge, however. We can think of two scenarios.

First, let's think about a small nation, like El Salvador, importing wheat from the United States. Imagine El Salvador slaps a 50¢ per bushel tariff on wheat imports. Who would end up footing the bill? It is tempting to argue that it would be the United States. After all, it is the trader who must pay to get the wheat into the country. But there is a big global market for wheat, and El Salvador is a small player in it. If the exporter can get

$5 per bushel for his wheat around the world, why would he accept a net payment of $4.50 from El Salvador? He wouldn't. The U.S. exporter will demand and receive $5.00, and the domestic price in El Salvador will have to rise to $5.50. The small country effectively pays the tariff, no matter who hands over the cash at customs.

Alternatively, think about a product for which the United States is the dominant consumer, such as leather American footballs. If a tariff raised the price to American consumers, they would likely decrease their quantity demanded. As a substantial portion of global demand, this would in turn drive down the global price. In the end, the burden is likely to be split between domestic consumers (paying more than before the tariff) and global producers (receiving less).

In either case, the tariff drove up prices in the importing country. This would not generally be welcomed by consumers, but it is to the advantage of domestic producers competing with imports. A U.S. producer of footballs would neither have to pay the tariff nor face such stiff competition from abroad. This effect is well understood by such industries as U.S. steel producers, who are among the most ardent seekers of tariffs against foreign competitors.

Imports are the difference between consumption and domestic production. That means that on an imported good facing tariff protection, the damage to domestic consumers—who see prices rise across the board—generally exceeds the benefit to domestic producers, and the country will be worse off. But domestic producers may be better organized than consumers and able to press their case successfully.[36]

The government will also reap some revenue, so long as the tariff does not completely discourage trade.[37] This, in fact, was one reason for the long-standing popularity of tariffs, going back centuries. If a country has only one or two major ports, it is far easier for a government to raise revenue by imposing tariffs than through trying to figure out everyone's income around the country and taxing that.

Aside from ease of imposition, however, tariffs are a relatively poor way for a government to raise money. They distort consumption decisions and impose a relatively large amount of economic pain for each dollar gained. As a general principle of taxation, the broader the tax base, the easier it is to raise funds with minimal harm. Thus, for efficiency, a tax on all consumption beats out a tariff that taxes only the consumption of imports.

QUOTAS

This is one reason why developed countries have drastically curtailed their use of tariffs, as we described in chapter 4. Developing nations have dropped tariffs as well, but they did so later and less thoroughly. Much of the protection in the world today takes forms other than tariffs. The most common of these is a quota, in which the government sets a numerical limit on the quantity of a good that may enter the country. Returning to our example of Salvadoran wheat imports, suppose the effect of the 50¢ tariff was to reduce annual wheat imports from twenty thousand bushels to ten thousand bushels (lower demand because consumers face a higher price). What if, instead, the Salvadoran government had set a quota of ten thousand bushels instead of applying a tariff? Would that have had the same effect?

Under certain conditions, it would. If the general conditions of demand and supply were unchanged, a ten thousand bushel limit on wheat imports would have made wheat relatively scarce within El Salvador. The price would rise until it hit a point at which ten thousand bushels just satisfies domestic demand. We already know that point occurs when El Salvador's domestic price is 50¢ above the world price.

One glaring difference between a tariff and a quota is that a tariff delivers revenue directly to the government. With a little creativity, a government can collect money through a quota scheme as well. For example, it could hold an auction for ten thousand permits, each allowing the holder to import a bushel of wheat. Those ought to be worth 50¢ each—the gap between the price in El Salvador and the price in the rest of the world.

Such auctions are not very common, however. If, instead, the government simply decrees that no more than ten thousand bushels will enter, then the money that would have gone to the government will go to whoever possesses the right to move those goods. That could land in domestic hands if importers are granted the right to shop on world markets. Or it could land in foreign hands if countries are just told how much of each good they are allowed to send.

This latter approach is far more costly to the country as a whole, and it is far more common. One long-standing protectionist scheme limited the quantity of textiles and clothing that could be brought into the United States. It assigned fixed quantities of knit shirts and underwear to each producing country around the world. The program operated for decades, but it was eliminated in 2005 as part of a global trade agreement. This gave economists an opportunity to study its effects. They found that in instances in which the quotas had constrained imports, the removal of the quotas led to plummeting prices. They estimated that the end of the program made U.S. consumers $7 billion better off.[38]

One remaining U.S. protectionist regime limits imports of sugar into the country. A study estimated that since 1982, U.S. sugar consumers have paid roughly 27.2¢ per pound compared to a world average price of 13.8¢ per pound.[39] Americans consume about 20.75 billion pounds of sugar every year, while U.S. producers turn out only 15.4 billion pounds. The study found that Americans would have saved almost $2.5 billion per year had they been allowed to trade freely at world prices.

These examples illustrate two other common points about protection. First, its costs may fall most heavily on the poor. They tend to consume proportionally more of the goods whose imports are restricted, such as food or

low-cost clothing. One preliminary study found that the recent rise of trade with China, by catering to the needs of the poor, had sufficed to offset by 30 percent the rise in U.S. measured inequality.[40]

The second point is that protection can have perverse consequences. The high price of sugar in the United States put a heavy burden on candy producers, some of whom closed their U.S. operations.[41] It prompted other heavy sugar users, such as soft-drink makers, to turn to a cheaper substitute—high-fructose corn syrup.

There are other sorts of protection beyond tariffs and quotas. One that recently leapt into the news was the "Buy American" provision in the 2009 U.S. stimulus legislation. It functioned something like a zero quota on government purchases of certain goods. It said certain stimulus funds could only be spent on goods produced in the United States or in countries with whom the United

States had an agreement on "government procurement." The market for government purchases can constitute 10–15 percent of all economic activity.[42]

What these various forms of protection have in common is that they limit the ability of consumers to seek out the best possible deal and thereby limit domestic competition; they favor certain domestic producers over consumers; and they frequently spur additional distortions in the economy.

All of the measures discussed in this chapter limited imports at the border. The next chapter takes up the issue of policies that operate behind the border but can nonetheless have a significant effect on trade.

7

**NOT YOUR FATHER'S
TRADING SYSTEM:
SERVICES, INVESTMENT,
AND THE ROLE OF
SUPPLY CHAINS**

The stereotypical image of trade usually begins and ends with manufactured goods, for example, automobiles the U.S. imports or computer chips the U.S. exports. But increasingly, throughout the last decades of the twentieth century, globalization has produced more complicated patterns of international commerce, such as increased cross-border trade in services and foreign direct investment. The new trade paradigm has also fueled new controversies over whether U.S. corporations are unpatriotic ("Benedict Arnolds," as Senator John Kerry [D-MA] argued in the 2004 presidential campaign) by abandoning their home country and sending jobs offshore through opening factories abroad. As we will see, however, in fact quite the reverse is true: foreign direct investment and new services trade increase growth, jobs, and, ultimately, U.S. living standards. First, though, let us review some basic facts.

SERVICES

The term "trade in services" was long thought an oxymoron. Services often require that producers and consumers be at the same place while the service is being performed: think barbershops and restaurants. But even before the recent revolution in communications and transportation, cross-border commerce in services was a common phenomenon. Service exports have included a domestic TV show or movie being shown in a foreign country or a doctor operating on a foreign patient. As for imports, think of a consumer who has a camera repaired abroad or a traveler who buys insurance from a foreign company.

There are several distinct ways in which cross-border services can be supplied.[43] The first mode (to employ the trade jargon) is similar to trade in goods: the service is sent across a border. As an example, consider a telecommunications transaction in which, say, a French company provides data services to a customer in Mexico. A second type of services trade requires the consumer to move abroad, as when a student or a tourist utilizes the services of a foreign university or hotel. The third, and possibly the most important and common provision of an international service trade, is through a commercial presence that is the result of foreign investment, for example, American Express establishing branches in many countries (55–60 percent of services trade is supplied in this manner). Finally, cross-border services can also be supplied through the temporary movement of workers. Examples could include construction workers or engineers at foreign building sites and/or management consultants who travel to a particular project.

While services can be supplied directly to final consumers, for international commerce there are strong umbilical ties between the manufacturing, agricultural, and mining sectors and business and professional services that are vital to any successful enterprise—including legal, accounting, data processing, transportation, banking, advertising, and insurance.

Services trade is estimated to make up about one-quarter of total world trade. This is almost certainly an undercount, as national and international statistics for services are notoriously fragmentary. In general, as economies become richer and climb the technology ladder, the service sector takes on a larger role. In developing countries, services constitute some 50–60 percent of the total economy. For developed countries, those figures rise to 75–80 percent.

The United States today is an advanced service economy. Service sectors make up almost 80 percent of the U.S. economy and provide jobs for almost 80 percent of U.S. workers. The United States is both the world's leading exporter of services as well as the leader in imports. In 2007, the last year before the worldwide recession skewed trade and investment statistics, total U.S. exports of private-sector services amounted to $480 billion; imports totaled $341 billion, resulting in a surplus of about $139 billion—continuing a consistent record of services trade surpluses (see figure 7-1).[44]

GLOBAL SUPPLY CHAINS

In chapter 2, one country made wool, one made looms, and they swapped. Modern commerce is more intricate and interwoven. There is a symbiotic connection between services, foreign direct investment, and the rise of global production and supply chains. There is a lot of cross-border investment, and the resulting linkages mean that the modern loom may be assembled from parts produced in a range of different countries.

FIGURE 7-1. U.S. CROSS-BORDER TRADE IN PRIVATE-SECTOR SERVICES: EXPORTS, IMPORTS, AND TRADE BALANCE, 1998–2007

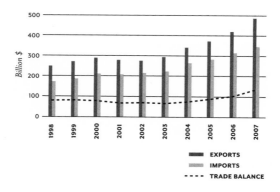

Source: U.S. Department of Commerce, Bureau of Economic Analysis, Survey of Current Business, October 2008, Table 2, available at http://www.bea.gov/.

From 1990 to 2006, worldwide inflows of FDI rose at an average of 12.4 percent annually, versus 7.7 percent growth in exports of goods and services, and investment flows have become a key driver of global economic growth.

The United States has been in the forefront of this new phenomenon. As with trade in goods and services, the United States (or more accurately, U.S. corporations) is both the largest supplier of foreign investment and the largest recipient. In 2006, U.S. corporations

FIGURE 7-2. MANUFACTURING SUPPLY CHAIN AND INPUT COSTS FOR THE APPLE COMPUTER IPOD, 2005

Source: Congressional Research Service, R40167, available at http://opencrs.com/document/R40167/.

invested just under $250 billion abroad, while foreign multinationals invested $195 billion in the United States (The total cumulative U.S. FDI abroad amounted to $2.4 trillion; total cumulative inward FDI to the United States was $1.8 trillion).[45]

Driving these large increases in cross-border investment is a new model for global competition that has resulted from dramatic, cost-reducing technological advances in communications and transportation, as well as public policies that have lowered trade and investment barriers (as described in chapter 3). What has emerged over the past two decades are multinational production or manufacturing supply chains that span the globe. Parts and components can be designed and commissioned in one location, manufactured in multiple locations, and assembled into a final product in other locations. As a study by the Congressional Research Service noted: "International trade now is less between countries than within a global supply network that may include headquarters, design, branding, and engineering in the United States, manufacturing in China, with parts from Singapore, Japan, and the European Union, and call center services in India." Figure 7-2 describes the supply chain for the Apple Computer iPod and list the inputs (value added) at each point in the process.[46]

Furthermore, as supply chains have multiplied, they have changed both what is being traded and by whom. Figure 7-3 demonstrates two important results: a boom for trade in parts and components as they may move across multiple borders on the way to a finished product; and a strong increase in the demand for commercial services to keep the supply chain moving efficiently. In addition, for U.S. multinationals, the rise of global competitive strategies has resulted in the increased importance of intrafirm trade with foreign affiliates. Over the past two decades, the share of U.S. exports shipped between U.S parent multinational companies to their affiliates has ranged between 50 and 60 percent of total exports, while

FIGURE 7-3. TRENDS IN WORLD TRADE OF TOTAL MERCHANDISE, INTERMEDIATE GOODS, AND OTHER COMMERCIAL SERVICES, 1988–2006

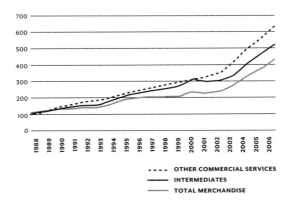

- - - - OTHER COMMERCIAL SERVICES
——— INTERMEDIATES
——— TOTAL MERCHANDISE

Source: World Trade Organization Annual Report 2008, http://www.wto.org/english/res_e/booksp_e/anrep_e/anrep08_e.pdf.

the share of imports from affiliates oscillated around 30 percent.

The rise of worldwide supply chains is also playing havoc with the way trade numbers are calculated. Gross figures for exports and imports of finished products disguise what's really going. A prime example can be seen in the trade between the United States and China. By official statistics, the United States ran a $226 billion trade deficit with China in 2009. The "Made in

China" label, however, hides the fact that many of the end products counted in the deficit (iPods, computers, telecommunications equipment) are composed of parts and components actually manufactured somewhere else. China has become a great assembling power and not—thus far—a great manufacturing power. This is particularly the case for high-tech products. Economists at the U.S. International Trade Commission estimate that one-half to three-quarters of the value of these end products come from abroad, mostly from China's more advanced Asian neighbors. Furthermore, of China's top two hundred exporting firms, 70 percent are foreign-owned or joint ventures. Thus, a sizable proportion of the country's giant export machine does not consist of homegrown products made by native Chinese companies, but rather of repackaged, high-value foreign elements.[47]

POLICY DEBATES

On the policy front, a hot debate has developed over the economic and social consequences of the new trade paradigm. Critics have argued that U.S. multinationals are, in effect, "abandoning" the U.S. economy and society, moving technology and jobs offshore.[48] Though it is true that the United States faces increased competition as more nations enter the global marketplace, and lower barriers to trade and investment increase the mobility of capital and technology, the dire predictions of antiglobal skeptics in general have failed to materialize. Indeed, quite the opposite is true: the activities of U.S.-based multinationals, both in this country and abroad, have increased U.S. productivity, competitiveness, and, ultimately, U.S. living standards.

In explaining why this is the case, we cite several facts and factors that are relevant. First, U.S. multinational companies are still overwhelmingly "American." As figure 7-4 demonstrates, U.S. parent corporations account for two-third of all worldwide U.S. multinational employment; about 70 percent of worldwide output; almost three-quarters of capital investment; and 85 percent of total research and development. With regard to the trade consequences, it is important to underscore that most sales by U.S. foreign affiliates do not come back to the United States: in 2007, U.S. foreign affiliates had total sales of $4.7 billion, of which only about $500 million came back to the United States as imports.[49]

On the other side of the coin, foreign direct investment in the United States further enhances U.S. growth, through adding to the capital stock and providing high-wage employment for U.S. workers. We should note that both parent U.S. multinationals and foreign-owned multinationals operating in the United States pay higher wages than purely domestic U.S. manufacturing plants (10–11 percent), based mainly on higher labor productivity and higher technological intensity.[50]

What, then, is the bottom line from all of this? Certainly outsourcing of jobs from the United States has long been occurring and will continue in the future. Call services—repairs, complaints, and magazine

FIGURE 7-4. U.S. PARENT CORPORATIONS AND WORLDWIDE ACTIVITY OF U.S. MULTINATIONALS

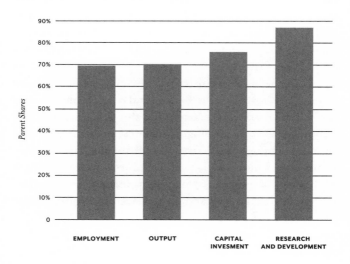

Source: Matthew J. Slaughter, "How U.S. Multinational Companies Strengthen the U.S. Economy: Data Update," United States Council for International Business, Washington, D.C., March 2009.

subscription renewals—are likely to be manned (and womaned) by Indian, Filipino, and Sri Lankan workers. But over against this reality is the fact that globalization and increased U.S. outward foreign direct investment have not produced a "hollowing" out of the U.S. economy. Overwhelmingly, the evidence demonstrates that, on balance, the expansion of U.S. multinational companies abroad and the strengthening of these same companies' operations in the United States are complementary: specifically what this means is that when U.S. multinationals invest more abroad, they export more from the United States and thus create additional U.S. jobs.

Nothing better illustrates the points and statistics assembled above than the history and current competitive position of IBM, perhaps the single most admired symbol of U.S. technological prowess over the past half century. Though the United States remains IBM's most important single market, it earns roughly two-thirds of its revenue abroad, with emerging markets such as China, India, Brazil, and Russia accounting for about 20 percent of revenue but growing fast. IBM's global reach cushioned the company from the recent deep recession in the developed world (United States and Europe) and has allowed it to take advantage of the steep growth rates recorded by developing countries over the past year. From 2006 to 2008, the company repatriated more than $20 billion in profits largely to reinvest in domestic operations.

IBM has also successfully converted itself from a major manufacturing giant to a services giant—though it still retains strong manufacturing capability, from transistors to supercomputers and nanotechnology. Business intelligence software and services in such fields as finance, energy, transportation, and resource and commodities management now produce 80 percent of IBM's revenue. Globally, it has been called the model of a "post-multinational" company. Though the high command is still located in the United States, IBM has set up global centers responsible for areas across the company: global purchasing and procurement in China; human resources in the Philippines; and back-office finance processing in Brazil.

Still, the brains of the company remain in the United States. In 2008, 70 percent of IBM's $6.9 billion in research-and-development spending was in the United States, and from 2002 to 2008, the company invested more than $11 billion in capital expenditures within this country. And though IBM is a truly global company, 25 percent of its workforce is in the United States.[51]

8

THE INSTITUTIONS OF TRADE: INTERNATIONAL AND NATIONAL

"GATT-zilla Eats Flipper," and "GATT-zilla Destroys Jobs," the posters screamed in Seattle, Washington, D.C., and Geneva in past years, as thousands of antiglobal demonstrators took to the streets to protest against the alleged predations of the GATT/WTO, run by "faceless bureaucrats" who work behind closed doors to trample social justice and undermine the sovereignty and rights of developing economies and societies. In truth, the WTO is both much less powerful and much more powerful than the NGOs proclaim—and fear. It is much less powerful because all decisions must be made by consensus (including the votes of developing countries) and the organization has no real enforcement arm. It is much more powerful, however, because increasingly it is looked to as the only multilateral body that has developed a body of laws and regulations that—largely through moral suasion—a vast majority of nations in the global trading system abide by.

The WTO is a "member-driven" organization, and national trade policy institutions form a necessary complement—as well as vital foundation—to the functioning and success of the organization. The United States has long occupied a predominant leadership role in the global trading system, and, thus, its trade policymaking institutions and the politics of trade in this country have exercised a strong influence on the GATT/WTO system since its founding in the 1940s.

ORIGINS OF THE MULTILATERAL TRADING SYSTEM

At the end of the Second World War, world leaders believed that there were strong moral and political, as well as economic, reasons to establish a multilateral system for global trade. First, they shared a common belief that trade protection and tit-for-tat retaliation had greatly deepened and prolonged the Great Depression of the 1930s. Furthermore, the postwar generation of political leaders also firmly held that the precipitous decline in international trade and investment had paved the way for the overthrow of democratic governments, the rise of authoritarian and totalitarian regimes, and, ultimately, the descent into war in 1939. They were determined to avoid these disasters in the future.

Ironically, plans for a powerful body to preside over global trade—the International Trade Organization— foundered on fears by the U.S. Congress that the new institution would infringe on national sovereignty (more on this continuing issue later). What survived was a tentative rump agreement called the GATT, which had been drafted as an interim set of rules and tariff reductions that would kick-start trade pending the creation of an international trade organization. For the United States, authority rested on the slender reed of a temporary congressional grant to the president for reciprocal trade concessions to nations that also agreed to tariff reductions. As time went on, this authority was repeatedly extended; but this also meant that the GATT never had a founding charter or formal organization.

Yet from this humble beginning and rudimentary organizational framework emerged one of the most successful international systems of the postwar era.

The brief GATT articles did include and embody two fundamental nondiscrimination principles that govern the multilateral trading system down to this day: unconditional most-favored nation and national treatment. The unconditional most-favored nation principle holds that a concession granted to one GATT member will automatically and without condition be extended to all GATT members. National treatment extends this rule domestically by mandating that once inside a member's border (after paying any legal tariff), foreign products and companies will receive the same treatment as domestic products and companies.

There were only twenty-three founding members of the GATT, almost all high-income developed countries. Over the past five decades, membership in the GATT (and now the WTO) has steadily expanded: the system now has 153 members, three-quarters of which are developing countries.

From the 1950s to the 1990s, under the aegis of the GATT, the members convened eight multilateral rounds of trade negotiations, the result of which was to reduce bound tariff rates from about 40 percent in 1945 down to about 5 percent today. Defining the success of the system, however, goes beyond the quite striking tariff numbers. Of equal importance is the large public good provided by the introduction of the rule of law and economic predictability into the international economic system.

First, developed countries and, increasingly in recent decades, developing countries benefited enormously by the secure knowledge that they would receive fair and equal treatment for their exports and international investments. As we have shown in earlier chapters, developing countries that opened up to trade and investment grew at a much faster pace than closed economies: part of this result stemmed from the assurance that the global trading system was steadily liberalizing and providing markets for new entrants into global competition.

THE WORLD TRADE ORGANIZATION

As time passed, however, it became clear that the institutions of the world trading system were failing to keep up with the increasingly complex issues that stemmed from regulatory barriers inside national borders that could impede trade and investment just as much as border tariffs. As a result, the early 1990s saw momentous changes in the institutions and the substantive rules of the game for international trade.

At the end of an extraordinary, wide-ranging round of trade negotiations in 1995 (the Uruguay Round, so-named after the nation where the negotiations were launched), a totally new structure, the WTO, was created, and the reach of international trade rules was broadened and deepened to include the services sector regulations; agriculture, health, and safety regulations; and intellectual property issues (patents, copyrights, and trademarks). Continuing a practice of the old GATT, the nations agreed that decisions within the WTO would be made by consensus (in effect they would have to be unanimous, or at least lack any vocal dissent), taken on the basis of one nation, one vote. Thus, the smallest WTO member nation has the same voting power as the largest economic powers.

Building on the still-valid most-favored nation and national treatment principles, a more effective system to settle disputes was established. Under the old GATT system, a nation accused of violating its obligations could block decisions that went against it. Under the WTO system, the decisions of newly established panels and the Appellate Body go into effect unless a consensus (in effect all members) of the WTO overturns the verdict. We should add, however, that WTO decisions cannot trump U.S. law. As with other nations, the United States can choose to ignore a ruling and opt to accept retaliation from other WTO members.

Despite the unfounded clamoring of northern NGOs, the WTO dispute settlement system is counted as a major advance and success (the "crown jewel" of the trading system). Between 1995 and 2010, some four hundred disputes have been handled by the new quasi-judicial system, and developing countries have accounted for about 50 percent of the complaints lodged.[52] Of equal importance, over the first ten years of its existence, the

WTO dispute settlement system achieved a compliance rate of 83 percent, far above the record of other international judicial systems and a strong affirmation of the power of moral and reputational suasion.

As a former director general of the WTO, Supachai Panitchpakdi—himself a citizen of a developing country, Thailand—stated on WTO's tenth anniversary: "The WTO…has extended the rule of law into the international trade realm and has contributed significantly to keeping peaceful and stable trading relations between WTO Members."

TRADE POLICY AND INSTITUTIONS IN THE UNITED STATES

Because of the central role played by the United States, U.S. trade institutions and politics have always exerted a potent force in the evolution of the global trading system. And fundamental to understanding the formulation and execution of U.S. trade policy is the fact that—almost uniquely among trading nations—the U.S. Constitution grants full authority for "interstate and foreign commerce" to the U.S. Congress. Unlike in other nations, where the executive often has a virtually free hand on trade issues, in the United States the elected representatives in the legislature hold the whip hand. This fact explains a number of key realities about the substance and politics of the U.S. system—not least that key congressional committees, Ways and Means in the House and Finance in the Senate, must agree to any significant policy initiatives in U.S. trade policy.

Furthermore, because of their access to Congress, powerful interest groups in the United States—the manufacturing and service sectors, labor unions, and environmental and consumer NGOs—can exert a more direct influence over trade policy than is usually the case in other trading nations.

Still, given the complexity of the contemporary trade agenda, and the fact that many issues have significant implications for regulatory policies (health and safety issues, services regulations, intellectual property), Congress has accepted that the president and his trade policy team must be granted enough authority to speak credibly for the whole nation. Indeed, for some decades U.S. trading partners have made it clear that they would not negotiate with the United States without assurances that final trade deals would not be vetoed by Congress or left hanging for years.

Under a compromise first reached in the 1970s, Congress decided that, if the president agreed to abide by specific instructions and if the executive kept Congress fully and currently informed regarding pending trade negotiations, it would agree to a process by which the president (and U.S. trading partners) were assured that Congress would vote on trade agreements without amendment and within a time certain. Though this agreement has recently come under fire from some members of Congress and outside interest groups, in the future there is no alternative to a new creative accommodation between the two branches if trade policy is to advance.

In the end, though each nation's system is somewhat different, trade policy is played out on two levels. First, national trade policies and priorities must be framed by the executive and then agreed to by the legislature, after listening to the voice of constituents. Then, U.S., or European Union, or Brazilian negotiators (as examples) must negotiate trade-offs with other WTO members in an attempt to reach compromises that balance multiple national goals. Then these same negotiators, backed by their presidents or prime ministers, must go back and sell the agreements to their elected representatives. It is a daunting process, but one that reflects both the broader span of the trade agenda and the impact of that agenda on diverse social, economic, and political domestic interests.

9

NEW ISSUES: LABOR AND ENVIRONMENTAL STANDARDS

As new patterns of global trade and investment have emerged, with effects that go deep into the social and economic fabric of individual nations, difficult questions have arisen regarding the reach and substance of the rules that govern the international trading system. These so-called linkage issues include, most important from a political perspective, trade and labor standards and trade and the environment. Specifically, should trade agreements, whether in the WTO or in bilateral or regional agreements, include regulations in these areas, accompanied by sanctions against countries that allegedly violate their obligations?

Skeptics of globalization, including developed-country labor unions, environmental organizations, student activists, and some human rights groups, argue that without such rules and sanctions, higher-income countries and their workers will be disadvantaged in competition with developing countries with lower standards. The result will be a "race to the bottom" as developing countries "unfairly" compete for jobs and investment, and high-income countries are pressured to lower their own labor and environmental standards. Furthermore, they argue that workers in developing countries are exploited by multinational corporations through abusive working conditions and suppressed wages.

Although the argument is superficially plausible, the major predicates on which the "race to the bottom" are founded empirically simply don't obtain. Given the advanced state of globalization today, one would have expected a "race" of foreign direct investment and jobs from the United States and other developed countries to low-income developing countries. Yet over the past several decades, FDI and trade flows have remained overwhelmingly between high-income countries. For the United States, even in recent years more than 70 percent of outward FDI by U.S. corporations has gone to high-standard, high-income countries such as Great Britain, France, Germany, Japan, Australia, and New Zealand. The forty-eight least-developed countries, which should have been the big winners in the race to the bottom, attracted less than 1 percent of all worldwide FDI.[53]

There are several reasons for these results. First, low wages alone don't give a determinative advantage to a developing country, fair or unfair. That is because low wages stem from low productivity, and, overall, workers in developed countries enjoy higher wages because they are more productive—through education, training, and more highly developed skills and know-how. With jobs, as with life, corporations have found that you get what you pay for. Second, when multinational corporations such as Toyota or Westinghouse go in search of new international investment opportunities, labor costs are only one of many factors they must consider. Nigeria has big market potential, but will political instability continue to dim its future? South Africa also boasts a large urban population, but will it ever develop the physical infrastructure to move goods for export?

Indonesia, finally, has enormous potential, but how long will it take for its educational system to produce basic skills and middle-level managers?

On a broader scale, numerous studies, starting with ones by the Organisation for Economic Co-operation and Development (OECD) in the 1990s, followed by academic analyses and later studies by the World Bank and the International Labour Organization, have found that low labor standards (unionization or the lack of broader social protections) are not correlated with either higher export performance or rising per capita income.[54] The OECD studies concluded, first in 1996 and later in 2000: "Empirical findings confirm the analytic result that core labor standards do not play a significant role in shaping trade performance. The view which argues that low-standard countries will enjoy gains in export market shares to the detriment of high-standard countries appears to lack solid empirical support."[55]

In fact, strong evidence suggests that those developing countries that have been more open to trade and investment not only have experienced higher growth than closed economies but also have raised labor standards as they attained higher per capita incomes. Thus, OECD analyses also concluded that the strongest finding is that "there is a positive correlation between successfully sustained trade reforms and improving core standards."[56]

At least part of the explanation for the linkage between trade and investment openness and rising living standards of many developing countries stems from the role of often-criticized multinational firms. Globalization skeptics accuse multinationals of exploiting workers through supporting sweatshops, paying very low wages, and trampling on labor rights.

Certainly it is true that one can find instances where economically powerful corporations have violated local laws and regulations and corrupted domestic politics and policies in developing countries. But the overall record—attested to by a vast majority of developing-country political leaders—belies this caricature so dear to the hearts of northern-based NGOs.

In the first place, jobs in foreign-owned affiliates (and domestic export industries) pay significantly higher wages than jobs in purely domestic industries. Academic research and work done by the U.S. International Trade Commission has established a "wage premium" of at least 10 percent paid by foreign multinationals (in some case the premium can go as high as 40 percent to 100 percent).[57] For Indonesia, for instance, recent research has established that for blue-collar workers the average increase was 10 percent, and the average increase was 20 percent for white-collar workers.[58] The point is that though wages in many developing countries are far below those of the United States or the European Union, the earnings of workers in multinational enterprises are much higher than the rest of the local labor market.

Similarly, multinational firms tend to bring higher safety and working standards and conditions to their workplaces than is likely the case for local establishments. As we have seen in many cases today, a factory in a developing country is part of a regionwide or worldwide production supply chain. And the multinational company at the head of that chain, for reasons of systemwide efficiency, has powerful incentives to set uniform standards not only for technical specifications but also for operating conditions. For example, Thailand is a top-ranked producer of processed foods such as tuna, chicken, shrimp, and pineapples, and it is a base for many multinationals, including Nestle, Unilever, Procter and Gamble, and Del Monte, among others. All of these companies have adopted international food safety standards as prescribed by the regulatory bodies of the U.N. World Health Organization and Food and Agricultural Organization.[59]

Douglas Irwin, a highly respected U.S. international trade economist, has provided a useful perspective on the debate over working conditions and multinationals: "Efforts to stop exports from low-wage countries, to prevent investment there by multinationals, or to impose high minimum wages or benefits beyond the productivity level of the domestic workforce will simply diminish the demand for labor in those countries and take away one of the few opportunities that workers have to better themselves and their families."[60]

Irwin's conclusions are particularly relevant, and poignant, in the debate over the imposition of trade sanctions and penalties for developing nations that allegedly violate labor standards. Both from a moral and economic perspective, there are major problems with this approach. First, sanctions inflict pain ultimately on the workers in a targeted industry—not on the government officials who dictate policy. By inhibiting growth in the targeted sectors, the sanctions will inevitably depress family incomes, leading to deprivation and a bleaker future. Furthermore, sanctions would most likely hit export-oriented sectors, which are generally the most productive in developing countries and which pay the highest salaries and enforce the highest standards. This would compound the difficulty of increasing national productivity and of raising living standards.

The situation has been starkly framed in the emotional area of child labor. Parents of children in Laos or Chad have the same aspirations for their children as parents in higher-income countries: schooling and the development of basic skills. But when the issue pits days in school against food from a dollar-a-day income, they have little choice but to send the children onto the streets to forage for basic sustenance.

Import bans on all goods produced with child labor could effectively stop those goods—but it would not end child labor and could well leave the children involved worse off. It has been estimated that only 5 percent of working children in developing economies are employed in export-related sectors: more than 80 percent toil in agriculture or for small local businesses and factories. Bans on exported goods, then, would have little effect on the larger child labor population and would likely push more of the children in the export sectors into more hazardous work at much lower wages. In a famous incident in Bangladesh, after a 1993 expose of child labor (under the age of fourteen) in garment factories, tens of thousands of child laborers were dismissed. It was later found that a vast majority of these children ended up in more dangerous, less remunerative jobs—breaking rocks, rolling cigarettes, and pulling rickshaws. A number of the girls ended up in prostitution.[61]

With regard to environmental standards, it turns out that as with labor standards, the story of the environment and trade does not fit any version of a "race to the bottom" theory. Over the past several decades, as total trade and trade between developed and developing countries has increased fourfold, environmental standards in developed countries have not eroded—in fact, the opposite is true. In multiple areas—air and water pollution, hazardous materials, chemicals and pesticides, acid rain, and deforestation, among others—pollution has declined, and developed countries have tightened environmental regulations. For instance, as a result of more stringent controls, levels of emissions for six common pollutants fell by 41 percent from 1990 to 2008 (see figure 9-1).

Furthermore, as they reach a certain level of development and technological capacity, virtually all developing countries have followed a path toward greater environmental protection. There is both an economic

FIGURE 9-1. AGGREGATE EMISSIONS OF SIX COMMON POLLUTANTS

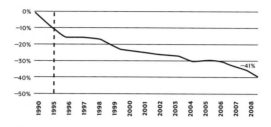

Source: Environmental Protection Agency, "Air Trends," www.epa.gov/airtrends/.

and social logic behind this progression. As expanding trade and investment creates higher growth and rising per capita incomes, countries move beyond subsistence spending, and environmental quality improvement is no longer a "luxury good." Environmental economists have identified a so-called Kuznets curve by which environmental quality in developing countries first deteriorates as a result of initial industrial development but then improves and rises as the country reaches a higher stage of development—and a more complex middle-class society where demands for a better quality of life (less air or water pollution) feed into the political process. Not all categories of pollution fit the pattern equally, but in general there is a consensus that environmental quality will rise with income (the threshold for the tipping point is in the area of $5,000 per capita GDP).[62]

As is the case with labor standards, environmental standards are not central to the locational decisions of multinational companies. It is estimated that environmental regulations add only about 1–2 percent to business costs in a given country. Furthermore, where possible, multinational companies maintain nearly uniform environmental standards in their domestic and host country plants. This allows them to benefit from economies in engineering standards for design, purchase, and maintenance; to reduce the potential for regulatory actions; and to avoid reputational damage in both local and international markets.

To conclude, we think that the best way to deal with potential market failure on both labor and the environment is to target the source of the market failure. For labor, this means attacking the domestic sources of poverty through education and training embedded within larger economic growth policies, including openness to trade and investment. For the environment, enacting and enforcing national environmental standards should be augmented with multilateral environmental regulations that nations have consented to enforce for themselves and for other nations in the international system. In both case, it is wrongheaded and self-defeating to attempt to utilize the trading system for sanctions that cannot reach and solve the underlying market failure and that ultimately reduce economic growth and living standards in developing countries.

10

CHALLENGES AHEAD

Trade has an impressive record of success in raising global economic well-being. It has been a cornerstone of U.S. national prosperity. Around the world it has helped raise hundreds of millions of people out of poverty. But it has been the subject of controversy throughout recent history. If anything, those controversies have mounted over time.

For years, the breakdown of global trade between World War I and World War II was seen as sufficient evidence of the dangers of protectionism. That experience helped motivate the great liberalization of trade that took place under the GATT and the WTO, the lowering of tariffs and quotas that had blocked international trade. Yet the memories of that period have faded, and the momentum for global trade liberalization has hit serious resistance.

Is that really so bad, though? After all, if tariffs have been substantially reduced in the developed world and effective institutions have emerged to settle trade disputes, what is so wrong about pausing to enjoy these gains and focusing on other issues for a while?

The question is whether the global trading system is sufficiently strong to weather a prolonged period without forward momentum. One reason that countries are willing to concede when they lose a trade dispute at the WTO is the value they place on that institution as a forum for negotiations. If that value seems to diminish because negotiations have stalled or died, there will be a temptation for countries, particularly strong ones, to ignore adverse findings and to flex their muscles on the global trading scene. In other words, the choice may not be between stagnation and progress but, rather, between progress and regress.

To conclude our discussion of trade, this chapter offers a guide to four main directions from which policy challenges to trade are likely to come in the near future.

Self-interest. Certain individuals and business profit from trade protection. We saw in earlier chapters that trade need not make everyone better off. Our imaginary wool vendor in Industria in chapter 2 did not welcome the fall in wool prices that accompanied a free trade agreement with Ruritania. In the United States, real-life sugar beet farmers and apparel manufacturers worry about imports from Latin America or China. We can argue that protection is a wildly expensive way to help these producers and that many are harmed to help a few, but those few have a very strong interest in avoiding global competition. They can and do organize and lobby to block imports.

Misplaced anger. The labor market in a dynamic economy like that of the United States can be daunting. Chapter 3 described the churn in the American labor market. This dynamism has generally served the country well, but it can be unsettling; it feels far less secure than an environment in which a worker holds a job for thirty years and then enjoys a reliable pension. The economy also seems to demand a steadily higher level of skill from workers in order for them to maintain a comfortable standard of living. The factory jobs that were once open to those with high school degrees are increasingly rare. Careful studies looking for the culprit usually attribute the economic shift to technological change, to domestic competition, and to international trade, generally in that order. But it is futile to rail against technological change ("Ban computer-guided machine tools!"), and those who do are derided as Luddites. It is pointless to object to domestic competition, as when textile jobs moved from the U.S. Northeast to the Southeast, because that competition is protected by the Constitution. That leaves international trade as the sole target for those frustrated with the challenges of modernity. It may not be the principal cause of their troubles, but at least it gives them a target for their anger.

Complexity. Chapter 7 described some of the ways in which trade issues have reached inside the border, as with increased trade in services. This can expand the gains from trade and bring about ever tighter integration between countries. But the complexity of modern trade and its reach into traditionally national domains can appear threatening. It can cause people to worry that they are being governed by "faceless bureaucrats in Geneva" and that they have lost the power to govern themselves. In addition to this backlash, more extensive integration means there are more issues on which something can go wrong. The United States has had homegrown-food safety issues, as with outbreaks of *E. coli*. These do not have the same resonance, however, as incidents of tainted food from China. No advocate of free trade suggests that a country must accept poisonous food or dangerous products. But here the issue of complexity reemerges. How do we know if a product is unsafe? There is strong scientific evidence that lead paint on toys poses a health risk. There is not the same evidence on health risks from genetically modified food. But European countries with protected agricultural markets have used safety arguments to exclude American grains. Whether this is protectionism or prudence requires a plunge into complicated scientific arguments.

Trade as a lever. Chapter 8 described the development of the system of global trade governance under the WTO. In some ways, the WTO has become a victim of its own success. It regularly performs the feat of getting countries to change their practices to comply with international rules. That sounds basic, but it's almost unique on the global scene. Neither the United Nations nor environmental organizations nor labor organizations have a particularly distinguished record of prompting compliance. In the case of trade, part of the WTO's effectiveness stems from the prospect it offers of retaliatory action; if the losing country in a dispute fails to change its ways, the winning country can slap on tariffs. This tool of international diplomacy lies nicely in between the extremes of military action (too drastic) and formal complaints (ineffective).

This means, however, that there is a strong desire to use the trade lever to move reluctant countries across the whole spectrum of international issues. Perhaps the most prominent of these on the horizon involves climate change. There have been serious proposals to levy tariffs on the products of countries that fail to adopt suitable environmental laws. Ostensibly, such measures would offset the cost advantages that come with lax rules, but it is hard to balance costs this way in practice. Costs differ because of a whole range of policies—education, infrastructure, taxation, and health care. The gains from trade described in chapter 2 did not depend on other countries, adopting proper environmental policies. Yet if there is a global problem, and international cooperation is proving difficult to achieve, trade leaps out as one of the few practical tools that can be used to prompt that cooperation. The danger is that if the trade lever becomes overburdened, it may snap.

These challenges—winners and losers from competition, the effects of modern technology and commerce, the complexity of economic regulation, and the potential to use trade policy as a device for altering other nations' behavior—all illustrate the point from which this book began. International trade shares the same benefits and blemishes of domestic commerce, but the opportunities for governments to intervene are more substantial in trade. That makes trade an early warning system for attacks on free enterprise and market-oriented economics in general, the proverbial canary in the coal mine. The unfortunate history of trade interventions presents a cautionary tale against succumbing to such attacks. The ability of an integrated world economy to lift people from poverty and let them do the work they do best is the strongest argument for free trade.

ENDNOTES

1 Angus Maddison, "World Development and Outlook, 1820–2030" (evidence submitted to the Select Committee on Economic Affairs, House of Lords, London, February 20, 2005), accessed November 22, 2010, http://www.publications.parliament.uk/pa/ld200506/ldselect/ldeconaf/12/12we14.htm.

2 Douglas A. Irwin, "Higher Tariffs, Lower Revenues? Analyzing the Fiscal Aspects of "The Great Tariff Debate of 1888," *Journal of Economic History* 58, no. 1 (March 1998): 59–72.

3 David Ricardo, *On the Principles of Political Economy and Taxation* (London: John Murray, 1817).

4 World Bank, World Bank Database, 2010, accessed November 15, 2010, http://data.worldbank.org/country/united-states.

5 Other things equal, countries tend to trade a lot with their neighbors.

6 Daniel Griswold, "Trading Up: How Expanding Trade Has Delivered Better Jobs and Higher Standards for American Workers," Trade Policy Analysis No. 36, Cato Institute, Washington, D.C., October 25, 2007.

7 Benjamin S. Bernanke, "Embracing the Challenge of Free Trade: Competing and Prospering in a Global Economy" (speech at the Montana Economic Development Summit, Butte, Montana, May 1, 2007).

8 Central Intelligence Agency, *The World Factbook* (New York: Skyhorse Publishing, 2009).

9 Dennis Tao Yang, Vivian Chen, and Ryan Monarch, "Rising Wages: Has China Lost Its Global Labor Advantage?" Discussion paper 5008, IZA Institute, Bonn, Germany, June 2010.

10 Douglas Irwin, *Free Trade under Fire* (Princeton, N.J.: Princeton University Press, 2002).

11 Claudia Goldin and Lawrence Katz, "Long-Run Changes in the U.S. Wage Structure: Narrowing, Widening, Polarizing" (paper prepared for the Brookings Panel on Economic Activity, Brookings Institution, Washington, D.C, September 6–7, 2007).

12 Cited in *Economic Report of the President 2008* (Washington, D.C.: Government Printing Office, 2008).

13 Scott C. Bradford, Paul L. E. Grieco, and Gary Clyde Hufbauer, "The Payoff to America from Global Integration," in C. Fred Bergsten, ed., *The U.S. and the World Economy: Foreign Economic Policy for the Next Decade* (Washington, D.C.: Peterson Institute for International Economics, 2005).

14 United Nations Conference on Trade and Development statistics, accessed November 22, 2010, http://www.unctad.org/Templates/StartPage.asp?intItemID=2068.

15 Jagdish Bhagwati, "Prebisch and UNCTAD," in Jagdish Bhagwati, *A Stream of Windows* (Cambridge, Mass.: MIT Press, 1998).

16 James Brooke, "International Report: Brazil Backing Computer Imports," *New York Times*, July 1, 1990.

17 Robert J. Barro and Xavier Sala-i-Martin, *Economic Growth* (Cambridge, Mass.: MIT Press, 2003).

18 Aaron Lukas, "WTO Report Card III: Globalization and Developing Countries," Trade Briefing Paper No. 10, Cato Institute, Washington, D.C., June 20, 2000.

19 David Dollar and Aart Kraay, "Spreading the Wealth," *Foreign Affairs* (September 2002): 120–33; David Dollar and Aart Kraay, "Trade, Growth and Poverty," *Economic Journal* (February 2004): 22–49.

20 Lukas, "WTO Report Card III."

21 World Bank, World Development Indicator, Washington, D.C., 2006, http://data.worldbank.org/indicator; see also Xavier Sala-i-Martin, "The World Distribution of Income: Falling Poverty and Convergence," *Quarterly Journal of Economics* 121 (2006): 351–97; and Shaohua Cehn and Martin Ravallion, "Absolute Poverty Measures for the Developing World, 1981–2004," World Bank Policy Research Working Paper 4211, World Bank, April 2007.

22 International Monetary Fund, "Regional Economic Outlook: Sub-Sahara Africa: 2008," Washington, D.C., 2008, http://www.imf.org/external/pubs/ft/reo/2008/AFR/eng/sreo0408.pdf.

23 Paul Krugman, "In Praise of Cheap Labor: Bad Jobs at Bad Wages Are Better Than No Jobs at All," *Slate*, March 20, 1997.

24 Ibid.

25 Allen Myerson, "In Principle, a Case for More 'Sweatshops,'" *New York Times* (Global Edition: Week in Review), June 22, 1997.

26 Nicholas Kristof, "Where Sweatshops Are a Dream," *New York Times*. January 15, 2009.

27 For a thorough discussion of mercantilism and objections to it, see Douglas A. Irwin, *Against the Tide: An Intellectual History of Free Trade* (Princeton, N.J.: Princeton University Press, 1996), particularly chapter 3.

28 Curtis P. Nettels, "British Mercantilism and the Economic Development of the Thirteen Colonies," *Journal of Economic History* 12, no. 2 (Spring 1952): 105–14.

29 Bureau of Economic Analysis, News Release, March 18, 2010, accessed August 25th, 2010, http://www.bea.gov/newsreleases/international/transactions/2010/pdf/trans409.pdf; "China's Current Account Balance Falls 35% in 2009," Xinhua, February 5, 2010, http://www.chinadaily.com.cn/bizchina/2010-02/05/content_9436621.htm.

30 Technically, there is one additional element: the change in foreign exchange reserves. For countries with market-determined exchange rates, this is usually unimportant. For China, it is very important. However, we can think of accumulated foreign reserves as just a variation on capital account IOUs.

31 Collateralized debt obligations (CDOs), in the form of chopped-up and bundled mortgages, played a major role in the financial crisis of 2008.

32 Bureau of Economic Analysis, News Release, U.S. International Transactions, June 17, 2010, accessed August 25, 2010, http://www.bea.gov/newsreleases/international/transactions/transnewsrelease.htm.

33 Philip I. Levy, "Doing a Job on NAFTA," *American*, March 6, 2008, accessed August 25, 2010, http://www.american.com/archive/2008/march-02-08/doing-a-job-on-nafta.

34 United States International Trade Commission Tariff and Trade DataWeb, accessed April 23, 2010, http://dataweb.usitc.gov/.

35 For a broad discussion of government interventions, see Philip I. Levy, "Imaginative Obstruction: Modern Protectionism in the

Global Economy," *Georgetown Journal of International Affairs* 10, no. 2 (2009): 7–14, accessed August 25, 2010, http://www.aei.org/article/101544.

36 The principal exception to this is if a large country can get a tariff just right. By driving down world prices, the country can get more imports for its exports and benefit from a tariff. This "optimal tariff" argument is subject to caveats, such as worries about other countries retaliating or about missing the optimal level. It would also require monitoring and periodic adjustment.

37 A tariff that blocks trade altogether is known as a "prohibitive tariff."

38 James Harrigan and Geoffrey Barrows, "Testing the Theory of Trade Policy: Evidence from the Abrupt End of the Multifibre Arrangement," NBER Working Paper 12579, October 2006, accessed August 25, 2010, http://www.nber.org/papers/w12579.

39 Mark J. Perry, "Sugar Tariffs Cost Americans $2.5 Billion in 2009," *Carpe Diem* (blog), accessed August 25, 2010, http://mjperry.blogspot.com/2010/01/sugar-tariffs-cost-americans-25-billion.html.

40 Christian Broda and John Romalis, "Inequality and Prices: Does China Benefit the Poor in America?" accessed August 25, 2010, http://www.freit.org/EIIE/2008/SubmittedPapers/John_Romalis.pdf.

41 Mark J. Perry, "American Sugar Prices Have Been Double, Triple or Quadruple the World Sugar Price," accessed August 25, 2010, http://www.umflint.edu/~mjperry/Sugar.htm.

42 Government Procurement, WTO, accessed August 25, 2010, http://www.wto.org/english/tratop_e/gproc_e/gproc_e.htm.

43 William H. Cooper, "U.S. Foreign Trade in Services: Definition, Patterns and Policy Challenges," CRS Report to Congress, RL31579, Congressional Research Service, Washington, D.C., April 7, 2009.

44 U.S. International Trade Commission, "Recent Trends in Services Trade: Annual Report," Publication No. 4084, USITC, Washington, D.C.

45 Raymond J. Mataloni Jr., "U.S. Multinational Companies," Survey of Currency Business, November 2008, Bureau of Economic Analysis, U.S. Department of Commerce, Washington, D.C; see also James K. Jackson, "U.S. Direct Investment Abroad: Trends and Current Issues," CRS Report to Congress, RS21118, Congressional Research Service, Washington, D.C., November 5, 2009.

46 Dick Nanto, "Globalized Supply Chains and U.S. Policy," CRS Report to Congress, R40167, Congressional Research Service, Washington, D.C., January 27, 2010.

47 Robert Koopman, Zhi Wang, and Shang-jin Wei, "How Much of Chinese Exports Is Really Made in China: Assessing Foreign and Domestic Value-Added in Gross Exports," Office of Economics, Working Paper No. 2008-3-B, U.S. International Trade Commission, Washington, D.C., March 2008; and Judith Dean, K. C. Fung, and Zhi Wang, "How Vertically Specialized Is Chinese Trade?" Office of Economics, Working Paper No. 2008-09-D, U.S. International Trade Commission, Washington, D.C., September 2008.

48 The Bureau of Economic Analysis in the U.S. Department of Commerce defines a U.S. multinational company as any U.S. enterprise that holds a 10 percent direct ownership stake in at least one foreign business enterprise. Today, there are 2,300

multinational parents that control about 24,000 foreign affiliates. To put this in perspective, under this definition U.S. multinationals represent less than 1 percent of all firms, but they exert an outsized impact on the U.S. economy. They generate about 20 percent of total U.S. employment and 25 percent of total U.S. output. See Theodore H. Moran, "American Multinationals and American Economic Interests: New Dimensions to an Old Debate," Working Paper Series WP 09-3, Peterson Institute for International Economics, Washington, D.C., 2009.

49 Matthew J. Slaughter, "How U.S. Multinational Companies Strengthen the U.S. Economy," The Business Roundtable and the United States Council Foundation, Washington, D.C., 2009.

50 J. David Richardson, "Global Forces, American Faces: U.S. Economic Globalization at the Grassroots," Institute for International Economics, Washington, D.C., 2005.

51 Slaughter, "How U.S. Multinational Companies Strengthen the U.S. Economy."

52 Many disputes never reach a formal ending with decisions by the panels or Appellate Body; about two-thirds are settled in the consultation and mediation phases of the process.

53 Daniel W. Drezner, "The Race to the Bottom Hypothesis: An Empirical and Theoretical Review," mimeo, The Fletcher School, Tufts University, December 2006.

54 In recent years, following definitions adopted by the International Labour Organization, core labor standards include the areas of child labor, forced (slave) labor, discrimination, and freedom of association and collective bargaining.

55 Organisation for Economic Co-operation and Development,

Trade, *Employment and Labour Standards: A Study of Core Workers' Rights and International Trade* (Paris: OECD, 1996), 12–13; Organisation for Economic Co-operation and Development, *International Trade and Core Labour Standards* (Paris: OECD, 2000); World Bank, "World Development Report: Workers in an Integrating World," World Bank, Washington, D.C, 1995.

56 Organisation for Economic Co-operation and Development, *Trade, Employment, and Labour Standards*; Organisation for Economic Co-operation and Development, *International Trade and Core Labour Standards*.

57 Mita Aggarwal, "International Trade, Labor Standards, and Labor Market Conditions: An Evaluation of the Linkages," USITC, Office of Economics, Working Paper No. 95-06C, June 1995.

58 Robert Lipsey and Fredrik Sjoholm, "Wages Spillover in Indonesian Manufacturing," *Review of World Economics* (2004): 321–32.

59 "Thailand: The Kitchen of the World," http://www.boi.go.th/english/why/Food_Processing.pdf.

60 Irwin, *Free Trade under Fire*, 215.

61 About ten thousand of these children were subsequently enrolled in special schools established by UNICEF, but this represented only a small fraction of the total number of children who had been employed in the garment factories; see *New York Times*, April 15, 2001.

62 Gene M. Grossman and Alan B. Krueger, "Economic Growth and the Environment," *Quarterly Journal of Economics* (May 1995): 353–77. For a thorough assessment of the challenges presented by trade and the environment by an author brought up in India but now a U.S. citizen, see Jagdish Bhagwati, *In Defense of Globalization* (Oxford: Oxford University Press, 2004).

Claude Barfield is a resident scholar at the American Enterprise Institute. His areas of study include international trade, science and technology policy, and intellectual property. He has taught at Yale University, the University of Munich, and Wabash College. He served in the Ford administration, on the staff of the Senate Government Affairs Committee, and was co-staff director of President Carter's Commission for a National Agenda for the Eighties. He received a BA from Johns Hopkins University and a PhD from Northwestern University.

Philip I. Levy is a resident scholar in economics at the American Enterprise Institute. He has taught international economics at Yale and Columbia universities. He served as Senior Economist for Trade for the President's Council of Economic Advisers under President George W. Bush and handled international economic issues as a member of Secretary of State Condoleeza Rice's Policy Planning Staff. He earned his doctorate in economics from Stanford University.